Cooking

From The

Heart *With*
Soul

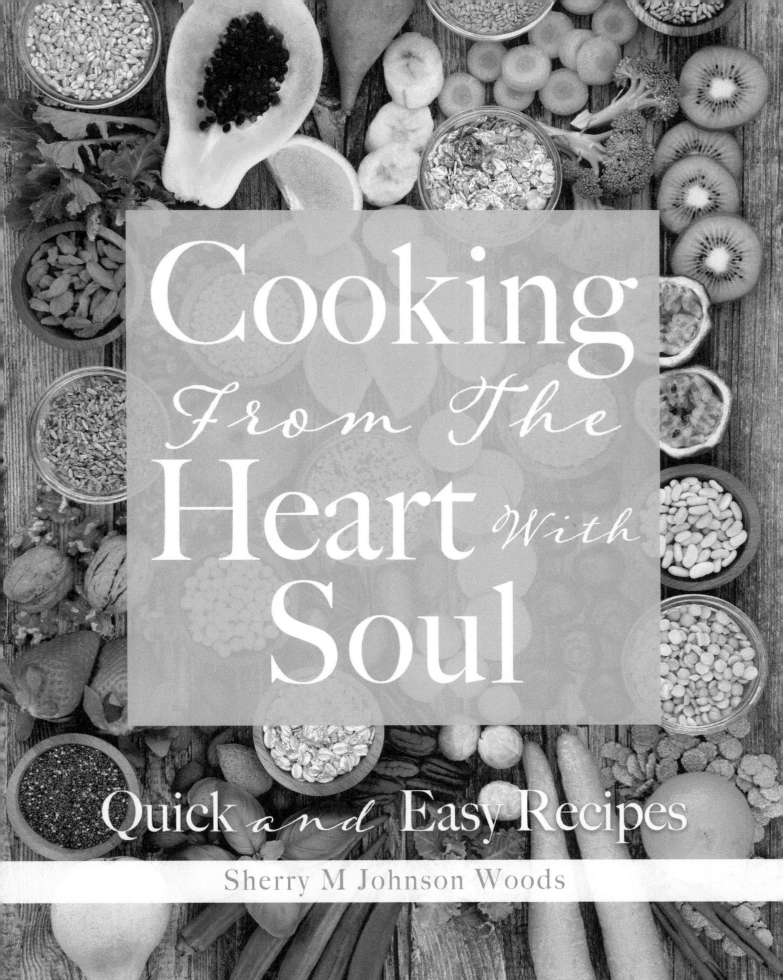

Cooking From The Heart With Soul

Quick and Easy Recipes

Sherry M Johnson Woods

Xulon Press
2301 Lucien Way #415
Maitland, FL 32751
407.339.4217
www.xulonpress.com

Paperback ISBN-13: 978-1-66281-627-7
Hard Cover ISBN-13: 978-1-66281-628-4
Ebook ISBN-13: 978-1-66281-629-1

TABLE OF CONTENTS

HELPFUL COOKING TIPS I LIVE BY

MAKING COOKING EASY STARTS WITH A CLEAN KITCHEN. Start with a sink of dish water to wash dishes as you go. You won't have much to clean up afterwards.

Have fun and don't be afraid to try something new, don't be intimidated. Cooking is like anything else; the more you do it, the better you will become. Take your time, don't rush, be patient. It's never too late to learn how to cook. Start with a dish and recipes that you love because that is the key to cooking. Cooking with love.

Take out time to read a recipe from beginning to end before you start your meal. A well written recipe is straightforward and easy to follow. Some recipes might take patience and reading multiple times before you can begin cooking. Have a pencil and paper with you to write down what you may want to omit or add to that recipe.

I was taught that there are two parts to a recipe: the list of ingredients and a list of steps that teach you how to make the dish. Most ingredients are in order of use in the recipe.

The sharper the knife the better they cut and it makes it not only easy to cut vegetables and potatoes, but easier on you.

Seasonings! Is there really a proper way... No, you like what you like but be careful not to over season especially when using salt and pepper. You should follow the recipe exactly the very first time. If you think more salt and or pepper is needed, update your recipe for the next time you prepare that meal. Don't be afraid to experiment with other seasonings: Paprika adds depth to rice and soups, Nutmeg enhances sauces and bitter greens and Cumin brings nice flair to meats and beans.

Eggs: The first thing I learned how to cook. I was 10 years of age watching my uncle Jesse. He had my attention while he baked a cake from scratch. He taught me to have fun, it's okay to make mistakes, don't be afraid, you control the temperature and the time, and until you know your oven and you are familiar with the meal you are preparing, never leave the kitchen until you are done.

I know of five preparations for eggs: My favorite, Over Medium, then there's Omelette, Boiled, Sunny Side up and Soft Scrambled. I love getting creative with scrambled eggs. I crack eggs into a bowl and whisk real good. Melting some butter in a skillet and cooking over medium heat, stirring often. I will toss and mix in several kinds of cheeses; cheddar, colby jack, mozzarella, parmesan, meats and vegetables mushrooms, tomatoes, jalapenos, red and green peppers, sausage, ham and bacon. Garnishing with picante sauce, parsley and chives. Sounds delicious? Create your own with what you like. Fun, easy and tasty.

My first Oven Baked Chicken, it was sooooo good. I now bake two at a time. Tips on baking a whole chicken; Season both sides and place the chicken on it's back in a baking dish. Stuff with butter and a medium size onion cut in half. Cover with foil and bake at 400 degrees for an hour and a half. Then uncover and cut a small slit down the middle if juice runs clear that is how I knew it is almost ready. Sprinkle paprika all over your chicken(s) and bake for another 10 to 15 more minutes or until they are done. Growing up we did not have a thermometer, if we did I didn't know what it was so I never used one. If you are using a thermometer, chicken cooks at 165 Fahrenheit.

If you are concerned about presentation, tie the legs together with kitchen string and put in the pan some garlic and lemon slices and garnish with some parsley flakes.

I never smash my Grilled Cheese Sandwich. There are a few tips for making a good melted sandwich with crisp bread on the outside and hot melted cheese on the inside.

Shredded or sliced cheese is okay, I heard grated and shredded cheese simply melts better and quickly than sliced cheese, but I use sliced cheese because that is what I normally keep in my fridge.

I butter my bread instead of melting butter in the skillet. Cook over medium heat ensures the cheese melts without over toasting the bread. Any cheese, meat, or vegetable can be layered into a cheesy melted sandwich.

Never smash your sandwich, this may cause your cheese to ooze out and flattens your bread. I like the fullness of my bread. You like what you like.

Shaking tips for a Cocktail; When making that drink, always measure out the ingredients and pour into a cocktail shaker, and then add ice. If you add ice before measuring, your drink may become diluted. After adding your ice shake vigorously for at least 30 seconds until there's condensation and pour into a glass.

Boiling great Pasta; I like to boil pasta with chicken broth instead of salted water. This will enhance the taste of your dish and cut down some of the sodium.

Here are a few items to have on hand.

Oven Mitts, plastic utensil for tasting and then you throw them away. Never double dip! Paper towels used to capture and drain oil from fried foods and use a paper towel to preserve vegetables, containers with lids to store leftovers in. Measuring cups, Measuring spoons, Wood spoons, Whisk, Spatulas, Tongs, Mixer, Blender. Skillets and pots in various sizes, Cake pan, Pot Holders,Cutting board or mat, Peeler and a good set of Sharp Knives. Try to keep frozen vegetables and meats (chicken breast, ground meat, catfish fillets) great for quick and unplanned meals.

Using seasoning such as; Garlic Powder, Onion Powder instead of Garlic Salt will cut your sodium intake down.

How to serve leftover soups with noodles, dumplings and or rice in them. Chicken broth used when serving leftover soups that have ingredients listed above that soaks up liquid. Yeees just add more chicken broth heat and serve.

Never put your Cast Iron Skillets in the dishwasher and always wash by hand. After washing dry then add a little of cooking oil and wipe with a paper towel, keeping them oiled prevents rusting.

Measuring Equivalents

1 Tablespoon = 3 Teaspoons

⅛ Cup = 2 Tbsp.

¼ Cup = 4 Tbsp.

⅓ Cup = 5 Tbsp.

½ Cup = 8 Tbsp.

⅔ Cup = 10 Tbsp. + 2 tsp.

¾ Cup = 12 Tbsp.

1 Cup = 48 Tsp.

1 Cup = 16 Tbsp.

8 Fluid Ounces = 1 Cup

1 Pint = 2 Cups

1 Quart = 2 Pints

4 Cups = 1 Quart

1 Gallon = 4 Quarts

16 Ounces = 1 Pound

MEATLESS BREAKFAST SANDWICH

Ingredients:
Coconut Oil(or vegetable oil)
2 Slices of Whole Multi Grain Bread
1 Egg
Tomato
Wholly Guacamole Minis cups (comes 6 cups in a pack) or make your own guacamole. Spicy or Original

Directions:
Toast bread (buttered lightly)
Spread the Guacamole on your toasted bread and set aside.

Heat a small amount of oil in a frying pan

Fry eggs over medium and place on top of the guacamole add sliced tomatoes and the other toasted bread on top of that. Slice your sandwich in half and enjoy!

BREAKFAST BAKE

Ingredients:
2 Packages Pillsbury Crescent Rolls
1 Roll of Owens Breakfast Sausage (Original or Hot) Cooked (Ham or Bacon of all meats of your choice. I use Sausage and Bacon
1 Bag of Frozen Spinach
1 Cup Shredded Mozzarella Cheese and or Cheddar Cheese
¼ Cup of Butter
½ Cup of chopped onion (optional)
⅓ Cup of Flour
1 Cup Chicken Broth
¾ Cup Milk
1/12 Cup of frozen Hash Browns
5 to 6 soft Scrambled Eggs
2 Tablespoons Milk

Directions:
Press Crescent Rolls in a 13x9x2 inch pan (bottom and the sides of the pan) Bake in the oven for 5 to 8 minutes until the crust is lightly brown. Then sprinkle some of your cheese on top of the crust.

For your filling saute onion in the butter add stir in flour,

Add Broth and ¾ cup of Milk all at once. Cook and stir over medium heat till thickened. Stir in cooked sausage(Ham or Bacon), potatoes, cooked eggs and heat on medium heat. Pour filling over cheesed crust. Separate remaining package of crescent rolls into 8 triangles. Cover Filling with triangles, brush with 2 tablespoons milk and some butter. Bake at 375 Degrees for 15 to 20 minutes or till the crust is golden brown.

ALMOST BREAKFAST OMELETTE

(Delicious!)

Ingredients:
Sliced Jalapenos
2 Eggs
Green Onions
1 Tomato
Salt & Pepper
Olive Oil or Vegetable Oil

Directions:
Cut up some green onions, slice or dice tomato

Heat 2 to 3 tablespoon of oil in a skillet, add your onions, tomatoes and jalapenos and cook on medium heat. Cook until soft and crack your eggs on top of the green onion, tomato and jalapenos, cook and flip (over medium).

OLD SCHOOL CINNAMON TOAST

Ingredients:
¼ cup butter room temperature
¼ cup sugar
1 teaspoon ground cinnamon
4 slices of wheat bread

Directions:

1. Preheat the oven to 350 degrees. Mix in a bowl butter, sugar, and cinnamon. The butter needs to be really soft, not melted.
2. Spread the mixture over one side of each of the 4 pieces of bread, cover all the way to the edge of the bread.
3. Place the bread on a baking sheet and bake it in the preheated oven for 5 to 10 minutes.
4. Then turn the broiler on and broil the toast until it is golden toasted and the sugar is bubbling. Great tip for this, leave the door of the oven slightly open to watch and make sure you don't burn it.

Enjoy!

GRILLED CHEESE SANDWICH

Ingredients:
1 Slice Colby Jack Cheese
1 Kraft Single Cheese Slices (Velveeta Cheese Slice)
2 Slices MultiGrain Whole Wheat Bread
Butter

Directions:
Spread butter on both slices of bread (only one side of each bread)

Place one of the slices of bread butter side down in a skillet on low heat. Add you slices of cheese on top and place the other slice of bread butter side up on top of that. Cook until golden brown and the cheese starts to melt. Flip the sandwich and cook until that side is golden brown. Best Grilled Cheese Sandwiches are the ones made with love and take your time cooking.

Add a slice of Ham or Turkey makes a great Grilled Sandwich as well.

BACON WRAPPED CHICKEN

Ingredients:
4 boneless skinless chicken breasts chopped into bite size pieces
12 slices of bacon
1 red, yellow and orange bell pepper cut into bite sizes

Sauce
1 tablespoon oil
2 teaspoons minced garlic
¾ cup ketchup
¼ cup brown sugar
⅓ cup apple cider vinegar
¼ cup honey
3 tablespoon worcestershire sauce
1 ½ tablespoons yellow mustard
2 teaspoons soy sauce
½ teaspoon chili powder

Directions:
Heat oil in a medium saucepan over medium heat. Add garlic and saute for 1 minute. Add all the remaining sauce ingredients and bring to boil. Reduce to a simmer and allow to cook over low until ready to use.

Wrap bacon around the chicken pieces, and add pepper pieces onto the skewers sticks. Brush sauce over skewers. Grill over medium heat 4-5 minutes, then rotate , brush with more sauce, and cook another 4-5 minutes until chicken is cooked through and bacon is crispy.. Use leftover sauce for dipping.

NACHOS MY WAY

Ingredients:
1lb Ground Meat
1lb Owens Hot Breakfast Sausage
I Block of Velveeta Cheese
2 Cans of Rotel Tomatoes
1 Can of Rotel Cilantro Lime
1 Can of Cream of Mushrooms Soup
1 Can of Cream of Chicken Soup
1 Small can of Chopped Green Chilies
1 Can of Cheddar Cheese Soup
1 Can of Fiesta Nacho Cheese Soup
1 Can of Wolf Brand Chili
1 Bag of Nacho Cheese Doritos Chips or Tostitos Chips

Directions:
Cook your Ground Meat and Owens sausage and set aside.

Dice the velveeta cheese into pieces and place in a microwave bowl, add all of the other ingredients and microwave for about 8 minutes. Remove and stir occasionally until all of the cheese has melted.

Garnish with Jalapeno Peppers

CRISPY AVOCADO FRIES

Ingredients:
3 avocados- ripe, not too ripe
Salt and Pepper to taste (Optional)
⅓- ½ cup of Flour
2 eggs
2 tablespoon water
½ to ¾ cups of Panko bread crumbs
(I sometimes use Cajun Fish Fry when I want a little heat)
Oil for frying

Directions:
Cut the avocados in half, then carefully remove the seed and cut through the avocado, not through the skin separating into 4 sections per half.(be careful when cutting that you don't cut through the skin.

Use a spoon to scoop out the avocado wedges from the skin, place on a plate and sprinkle a little salt and pepper (optional)
Pour the flour on a plate, then coat each slice well with flour and remove to another plate.
Beat eggs in a bowl well with the water.
Put the bread crumbs in the same kind of bowl.
Dip the floured slices of avocodas into the egg mixture, then roll quickly in the bread crumbs. (Add more bread crumbs as needed).

Heat oil in a large frying pan enough to cover battered avocado wedges. Drop wedges carefully into the oil as many as you can without them touching and cook for about 45 seconds before turning with a fork and cooking until crispy and golden brown. Remove from oil and place on a paper towel to drain oil.

Ranch Dressing for dipping or enjoying by themselves.

GIGI'S FRIED BREAD

Ingredients:
1 Box of Jiffy Corn Muffin Mix
1 Egg
Corn Meal
Milk
Crisco Vegetable Oil
1 Large Bowl
1 Skillet
1 large spoon
spatula

Directions:
Pour Jiffy Corn Muffin Mix in a large bowl
Pour in ¾ cup of cornmeal and stir well
Add egg and ¾ cup of milk and stir well

Heat Vegetable oil in a frying pan spoon cornbread mix into desired patty sizes fry and flip. Depending on your sizes this batch can make up to 12 patties.

Enjoy! So good and a change from regular cornbread. Reminds me a lot of mommy's hot water cornbread, Yummy

MOMMY'S FRIED SALMON PATTIES

Ingredients:
1 can of Pink Salmon
1 to 2 Eggs
Saltine crackers
½ lemon
1 Onion
Parsley Flakes

Directions:
Drain liquid from the can of Salmon into a separate bowl.

Place salmon in another bowl. Pull salmon apart and remove all the bones.

Squeeze the lemon juice over the salmon, add eggs, crumble some crackers and add 1 tablespoon of parsley flakes and mix together by hand well. Season to taste with Lawry's Seasoning Salt, Garlic Powder and Black pepper to taste.

After you finish mixing together well add 2 tablespoons of the juice from the salmon and diced or chopped onions and mix well.

Heat some cooking oil and form a nice size of your salmon into a patty and fry golden brown.

FIESTA SALAD

Ingredients:
1 pound ground beef
1 package taco seasoning
1 Onion chopped
Lettuce shredded
Tomato cut to desired bite size
1 avocado peeled and pitted (sometimes I use guacamole) Fiesta Shredded Cheese (2 packages if you want more cheese) 1 can of black beans drained (optional)
1 can of Whole Kernel Corn drained (optional)
White Rice (Cooked until tender) I use a bag of 1 minute rice Picante Sauce Fritos Corn Chips

Directions:

1. Prepare the ground beef with chopped onions as directed by the taco seasoning package and drain off grease.
2. Boil the rice drain and set aside

Serve in a bowl or on a salad plate. Pour some fritos corn chips first, then spoon some rice over corn chips, add some ground beef, shredded cheese, beans, corn, lettuce and tomatoes top off with some sliced avocado and some picante sauce.

SPINACH & BROCCOLI SLAW SALAD

Ingredients:
2 cups baby spinach
6 oz baby carrots
2 tablespoon olive oil
½ tablespoon lemon juice
½ teaspoon black pepper
2 heads of broccoli
½ red onion
½ tablespoon vinegar
1 teaspoon salt
1 avocado, sliced (optional)

Directions:
Cut broccoli (cut off stems) into florets and place in a large bowl
Add the spinach and mix
Add avocado, carrots and sliced onions to the bowl with the broccoli and spinach

In a separate small bowl prepare the dressing by mixing the olive oil, vinegar, lemon juice ,salt and pepper until well blended.

Pour the dressing over the salad and mix well. (make and add more dressing as needed)

SAUSAGE STUFFED JALAPENO PEPPERS

Ingredients:
Whole Jalapeno Peppers
1 Regular size of Owens Breakfast Sausage 1 Philadelphia Cream Cheese
1 Bag of Shredded Parmesan Cheese
1 Bag of Shredded Mozzarella Cheese
1 Bag of Shredded Mild Cheddar Cheese

Directions:
In a nonstick pan cook sausage. Then reduce heat and add cheese(s) stirring and mixing well with a wooden spoon.

Slice peppers in half long ways and remove seeds. I use gloves when I slice and remove the seeds.

Spoon mixture (or use your fingers)and fill the sliced peppers and place in a baking pan or cookie sheet. Bake uncovered at 350 degrees for 10 to 15 minutes.

For deep frying make a thick cornmeal batter with eggs. Heat oil in a deep fryer on high and roll stuffed peppers in the batter and place in the deep fryer. Remove once crispy and golden brown.

FRIED SQUASH

Ingredients:
1 Medium size squash thinly sliced
Pancake or waffle mix
Salt to taste

Directions:

1. Prepare pancake mix per instructions on the box, in a bowl
2. Dip the squash in the batter and place evenly in the air fryer.
3. Fry them in the air fryer on 390 degrees for about 5 minutes on each side or until they are crispy. Salt lightly to taste.

For frying oil, heat oil and place breaded quash in a frying pan or a deep fryer cook until golden brown. Salt optional.

CREAMED SPINACH

Ingredients:
2-8 oz bags frozen chopped spinach
2 ½ tablespoon butter
½ onion chopped
2 cloves garlic, minced
½ cup milk
¼ cup heavy cream
4 oz. cream cheese (½ of 8 oz cream cheese)
Salt
Pepper
Pinch cayenne pepper (optional)
¼ cup grated parmesan cheese

Directions:

1. Melt the butter over medium heat, add onion and cook until soft. Add garlic and cook for 1 more minute.
2. Add milk, heavy cream and cream cheese to the skillet. Simmer and stir until cream cheese is melted. Season with salt and pepper and pinch of cayenne pepper to taste.
3. Add spinach and parmesan cheese and let simmer stir and serve.

PARMESAN MAC AND CHEESE

Ingredients:
8 oz elbow noodles or pasta of your choice
2 tablespoon unsalted butter
2 tablespoon all purpose flour
½ cup and 2 tablespoon 2% or low fat milk
1 tablespoon or 3 large garlic cloves
1 cup heavy cream
1 cup shredded Parmesan cheese
½ cup shredded mozzarella cheese
½ teaspoon garlic powder
Ground pepper to taste(optional)

Directions:

1. Boil pasta until tender. Drain and set aside.
2. In a saucepan, add ½ cup milk and garlic, simmer for a few minutes until garlic softens. Then set aside.
3. In another saucepan, add butter on low heat until butter is melted. Add in flour and whisk until smooth. (if using garlic cloves remove garlic clove from milk and then add 2 tablespoon of milk. Also add in heavy cream. Parmesan cheese, mozzarella cheese, and garlic powder. Bring the saucepan to medium heat. Whisk and stir until the cheese is melted and smooth.
4. Add cooked pasta stir until pasta is coated with the cheese sauce.
5. (if you want a top cheesy crust add shredded mild cheddar cheese on top in a casserole dish and place in the oven 350 degrees and bake until cheese is melted).

CROCKPOT POTATO SOUP

Ingredients:

5 pounds peeled potatoes cut up (cubed 8 cups) 1 chopped onion

5 cans chicken broth (14.5 oz can)

½ teaspoon minced garlic

1 ½ teaspoons salt

¼ teaspoon pepper

2 packages cream cheese softened and cubed 1 cup half and half cream

1 cup of cut up butter

1 pound cooked and crumbled bacon

¾ cup shredded sharp cheddar cheese

¼ cup minced chives

Directions:

1. Place potatoes and onion in a slow cooker, add broth, garlic, salt, and pepper. Cook covered on law 8 to 9 hours or until potatoes are tender.
2. Mash potatoes to desired consistency, Stir in cream cheese, half and half cream, and butter. Cook, covered, 15 minutes longer or until heated through.
3. Stir soup to combine all ingredients, Garnish with bacon, cheese and chives.

(Try this with cubed chicken and broccoli)

DELICIOUS!

CHEESEBURGER SOUP

Ingredients:
1 lb ground meat
1 c chopped onions
5 T butter
¾ c chopped celery stalk
1 c shredded carrot
1 t dried parsley
2 cans of chicken broth
3 ½ c diced potatoes
¼ c flour
1 ½ c milk
8 oz cheese -Velveeta diced
½ t each of salt and pepper

Directions:
Brown ground meat and onion in a large skillet/pan over medium heat. Drain: set aside. In the same skillet saute celery carrots parsley and basil and 2 T butter. Until tender, add chicken broths"; bring to a boil. Add diced potatoes and beef; simmer 10 - 12 minutes, In a small skillet melt the 3 T butter, stir in flour until paste forms. Whisk in milk; cook until thickened and smooth. Add this to the soup; bring to a boil one more time. Add seasonings and cheese,, cook on low until melted. Serve hot!

TACO SOUP

Ingredients:
1lb Ground meat
1 Onion
1 Package Hidden ValleyThe Original Ranch Salad Dressing & Seasoning Mix 1 Package of Taco Seasoning Mix
3 cans of Ranch Style Beans
1 can of Italian Stewed Tomatoes
1 can of Original Rotel
2 cans of Whole Kernel Corn

(Optional) Garnish with Sour Cream, Jalapeno peppers, Fiesta Shredded Cheese, Sliced Avocado and some Nacho Cheese flavor Doritos.

Directions:
Cook your ground meat and chopped onions in a skillet. (Do not season meat). Drain off fat and spoon into a pot on medium heat then add all of the canned items (do not drain juice) , slice the italian stewed tomatoes in fours. Pour in your Taco Seasoning and Ranch dressing stir well over medium heat.

(Optional) Garnish with Sour Cream, Jalapeno peppers, Mild Cheddar Cheese, Sliced Avocado and some Nacho Cheese flavor Doritos.

OXTAIL STEW

Ingredients:
Lawry's Seasoning Salt
Garlic Powder
Accent
Pepper
3 to 4lbs Oxtails
1 large Onion
2 cans of Italian Stewed tomatoes
4 potatoes
2 Cans of Corn
1 Can of Italian Green Beans or Cut Green Beans
1 Can of Green Peas
3 Carrot sticks or 1 can of Diced Carrots

Directions:
First rinse off Oxtails

Fill a pot with water to boil Oxtails lightly add Seasonings, Oxtails, Onion (cut into fours) add 1 can of Italian Stewed tomatoes and juice, cutting the tomatoes in half and boiling until oxtails are tender.
If your water cooks out add more as needed. This is your broth no need to add tomato sauce, While your Oxtails are cooking, peel and dice the carrots and potatoes, rinse with water. Add to the pot once the oxtails are tender. Reduce heat and open and drain all canned vegetables or (fresh vegetables) add cook until tender. Then add the last can of tomatoes if needed optional.
This recipe can also be prepared in a crockpot. Let your Oxtails cook until tender in the crockpot and then add all vegetables and potatoes cook until soft. Season to taste.
You can also make this using Stew meat instead of Oxtails. (Beef Stew my way)

BURGER DOGS

Ingredients:
1lb of Ground meat
1 Pack of Ball Park Beef Weiners
1 Package of Hamburger Buns
1 Can of Manwich Original Sloppy Joe Sauce
1 Large Onion
Butter to Saute Onions

Directions:
Cook ground meat and drain fat.
Prepare Manwich by the direction on the can adding the ground meat
Slice onion and add butter to another skillet and saute the onions.
Remove the onions from the skillet

Split your wieners down the middle but not apart. Add more butter in the skillet and cook the weiners on both sides, add more butter and grill your buns.

Place one of the weiners on your bun spreaded apart. Spoon some of the manwich on top of the weiners and top with the grilled onions.

This is one of my family's favorites.. I serve this one with some Lay's potato chips or with some slow fried potatoes and onions.

MEATLOAF

Ingredients:
3 eggs
⅔ cup crushed saltine crackers
½ cup chopped onion
½ cup of chopped green bell pepper
1 ½ pounds lean ground beef
2 can of Hunts Seasoned Tomato Sauce for Meatloaf ½ tablespoon of Ketchup
Butter to saute onions and green bell pepper
½ teaspoon of brown sugar (white sugar okay too) Garlic Powder
Accent
Lawry's
Pepper

Directions:

1. Preheat the oven to 350 degrees. Saute onions and green bell pepper.
2. In a large bowl, put the eggs, saltine crackers, onion and bell peppers and the ground meat. Mix well with your hands thoroughly.
3. Add 1 can of the meatloaf tomato sauce, sugar and ketchup. Mix well.
4. Lightly season with garlic powder, accent, Lawry's and pepper (optional) Mix with hands real good and shape into a loaf in an ungreased baking pan or loaf pan.
5. Bake for an hour and pour grease if any off and add the last can on meatloaf sauce over the top and back until done. You will know if the meatloaf is done if the liquid is running clear, or cut in the middle to make sure your meat is cooked all the way through.

ROTEL CHICKEN SPAGHETTI

Ingredients:
3 boneless, skinless chicken breasts
Chicken Broth
1 can cream of chicken soup (10.75 oz)
1 can cream of mushroom soup (10.75 oz)
1 Rotel with green chillies (10 oz)
1 clove garlic, minced
1 onion diced
Celery
1 bag of Mild Cheddar cheese
2 tablespoon butter
Salt and Pepper to taste (I use Lawry's Season Salt) 1 8 oz block Velveeta cheese, cubed
8 ounces spaghetti, cooked and drained

Directions:

1. Preheat oven 350 degrees
2. Boil chicken and ½ of the onion diced, remove from broth and let cool, set broth aside and cut chicken into bite size pieces or shred.
3. Melt butter and saute the rest of the onion and two celery sticks diced over medium heat.
4. Poor noodles in a casserole dish,(or foil pan) and add all the ingredients, (sauteed onions, celery, cubed velveeta, soups, rotel tomatoes with green chilies).
5. Season to taste and stir with a large spoon add 2 cup of chicken broth.
6. Cover with foil and bake for 30 minutes at 350 degrees or until the cheese has melted and heated through. 7. Remove from the oven stir and mix well and sprinkle Mild Cheddar cheese over the top, place back in the oven uncovered for about 10 minutes or until the cheese melts.

PEPPERONI SPAGHETTI

Ingredients:
1pound lean ground meat
2 to 3 jars of Ragu Chunky mushrooms spaghetti sauce (or mix with one Sauteed Mushrooms)
1 can of Italian stewed tomatoes(I cut up my tomatoes) Spaghetti (I use thin spaghetti)
1 to 2 Green Bell peppers cut into desired pieces 1 large onion chopped or cut into desired pieces
1 Tablespoon butter
Garlic powder
Black Pepper
Accent
Lawry's Seasoning Salt
Pepperoni Slices
Eckrich Sausage (I use Skinless)
Parsley Flakes

Directions:
Break up ground meat in a skillet over medium heat, season to taste with seasonings, add butter onion, bell pepper, sliced eckrich sausage and pepperoni slices. Cook and stir until meat is brown and vegetables are tender. Drain grease

Cook the spaghetti to the package directions. Drain water and sit aside or mix in with the spaghetti sauce mixture. (I like to spoon meat sauce over my noodles.

Garnish with shredded parmesan cheese or cheddar cheese and parsley. Enjoy with garlic bread and a leafy salad.

GOULASH

Ingredients:
½ Pound of Ground Meat
1 Bell pepper
1 Onion
1 cup of Large Elbow Noodles
1 can of Italian Stewed tomatoes
3 cans of Tomato Sauce
Mild Cheddar Cheese (I use Kraft Cheese slices)
Lawry's Seasoning Salt
Garlic Powder
Accent
Pepper

Directions:
Boil noodles until softened and strain the water. While noodles are cooking, cook ground meat seasoned to taste. Pour off grease, add chopped or sliced bell pepper and onions to the ground meat and cook on medium heat until softened.

Pour noodles, tomato sauce and ground meat in a baking pan. Stir with a large spoon and add stewed tomatoes and juice. Slice tomatoes in half or in fours and and stir. Smooth out and place cheese slices on top or you can sprinkle Mild Cheddar Cheese over the top and bake until the cheese is melted. Add more tomato sauce if needed.

Serve alone or serve with Green Beans or Broccoli and cornbread

Double ingredients for a larger serving.

SHERRY'S QUICK CHICKEN AND DUMPLINGS

Ingredients:
Chicken parts of your choice (I use 4 skinless chicken breasts and two thighs).
1 Onion
Pillsbury Breakfast Biscuit 2 to 4 cans or Flour Tortillas Chicken Broth
1 stick of Butter
Chicken Bullions or Lawry's Seasoning Salt, Pepper, Garlic Powder, Parsley Flakes and Accent.

Directions:
Boil your chicken, onions and seasonings in a pot until done. Take your chicken out and set aside to cool. While your chicken is cooling turn the heat down. Then add 1 stick of butter to the broth from boiling your chicken and pull apart your biscuits or tortillas in bite size or larger pieces and add to your chicken broth. Once your chicken has cooled, pull the meat from the bone into the size pieces you want. Add your chicken to your broth and add more onions and seasoning to your taste. Your dumplings will soak up some of your broth, so add more chicken broth as needed. Stir to keep from sticking.

CHICKEN POT PIE

Ingredients:
4 cups cut or shredded cooked chicken
4 cups diced potatoes or frozen cubed potatoes
1 package of frozen mixed vegetables or can drained
1 can of cream of chicken soup
1 can cream onion soup
1 cup of milk
1 cup of sour cream
2 tablespoons of flour
¼ teaspoon garlic powder
½ teaspoon salt
½ teaspoon pepper
1 box of pillsbury pie crust (2 crust to the box)
Deep Dish Pie Crust (2 in a pack)

Directions:
Preheat the oven to 400 degrees, Combine the ingredients and divide put in the 9 inch deep dish pie plates.

Roll out the crusts to fit top of each pie. Place over filling; trim, seal and flute edges by pinching. Cut slits on top . Bake until golden brown 35 to 40 minutes. Cover edges with foil around edges to keep the edges from browning too fast to prevent burning.

You can also use smaller foil pans

CREAMY CHICKEN AND RICE

Ingredients:
Chicken parts of your choice (I use Chicken wings, thighs and breasts)
1 bags of Yellow Rice 5oz. (I like to use the Mahatma Saffron Yellow seasonings Long Grain Rice)
2 to 3 cans of Cream of Mushroom Soup
Butter or some non-stick spray (I butter my casserole dish)
Lipton Onion soup mix

Directions:
Butter the bottom and the sides of a casserole dish, next sprinkle the rice on top of the butter, place your pieces of chicken on top of the rice, spoon and spread the cream of mushroom soup(1 to 2 cans, depending how much chicken or the size of your pan) all over the top of the chicken and then pour a package of the Lipton Onion soup mix over it all. Fill one of the empty cans of cream of mushroom with water, pour all over the ingredients in the dish, use a fork to lift the chicken so the water can get under the chicken to the rice. Repeat with the water if 1 can of water is not enough. Cover with foil and bake at 375 to 400 degrees for about 1 1//2 hours or until the chicken and rice is done. Check under the pieces of chicken make If your rice is not done (soft) place back in the oven adding more water if needed.

One of my favorites. Serve with a salad or broccoli .You can also make this meal with Pork Chops as well. I have done one half of my casserole dish with my choice of Chicken parts and the other half of the casserole dish with Pork Chops.

CHICKEN AND SHRIMP PEPPERONI

Ingredients:
1 lb boneless skinless chicken thighs
9 16-20 count shrimp about ½ lb
1 small red bell pepper seeded and sliced
8 oz mushrooms sliced
2 oz pepperoni sliced
Garlic salt
8 oz can of chicken broth
2 oz marinara sauce or ragu with mushrooms
¼ cup grated Romano cheese
1 tsp chopped Italian parsley
1 pinch of crushed red pepper flakes
seasoned flour (seasoned salt and pepper)
1 tbsp of butter
1 lb linguine or thin spaghetti

Directions:
Heat a large Saute pan, then add Butter and or Olive oil.
Place your chicken thighs in the seasoned flour and add to hot oil. Let chicken cook for 2 minutes until done on one side and has a little color, then turn over and add sliced peppers, and mushrooms.
Continue to saute for 4 or 5 minutes, mixing ingredients until the peppers and mushrooms start to cook. Add the shrimp and continue to cook until, shrimp are almost fully cooked.
Now add the chicken broth, marinara, Romano cheese and red pepper flakes. mix well.
Remove the shrimp from the pan and add the pepperoni slices 3 -5 minutes. on low heat
Remove the pan from the heat and add the shrimp back into the pan
Cook your pasta per instructions on the box.

Two minutes before your pasta is done, start to heat your Chicken and Shrimp Pepperoni, roll butter in seasoned flour, and add to pan to thicken sauce
Continue to heat on medium heat as you drain your pasta.
Serve the chicken and shrimp pepperoni on a bed of linguine.

(If your sauce appears too thick or oily, add more water to it, this will thin it out.)

Notes

You will see more oil in this dish then you probably want, but this comes from the pepperoni. Drain some of the oil if you need too.

EASY CHICKEN DINNER

Ingredients:
Chicken (I like chicken wings and chicken breast) You can use any part of the chicken you like.
Carrots
Potatoes
Broccoli
Onion (s)
Butter
Lawry's Seasoning Salt
Garlic Powder
Accent
Pepper
Parsley Flakes

Directions:
Butter a casserole pan or a foil pan. Rinse off your chicken with water and place evenly in the bottom of the pan and lightly season. Then cut carrots, slice or dice onion(s) peel potatoes (skin on optional) and cut into fours. Layer vegetables and lightly season again, add butter throughout the pan.

Cover with foil and bake on 400 until your meat and vegetable are done. Cook your broccoli and serve with your meal.

This meal is good with pork chops or make it a Vege meal.

CHOPS THE RANCH WAY

Ingredients:
4 Pork Chops
1/2 cups of Milk
1 Egg
1 Packs of Hidden Valley Ranch Salad Dressing Seasoning Mix
1 cup All Purpose Flour
Pepper
Crisco vegetable oil

Directions:
Pour flour in a nice size bowl, whisk in the milk, egg, ranch seasoning and a pinch of pepper. Your batter should be thick enough to coat your pork chops. If too thin add more flour if too thick add more milk. Set your batter aside.

Heat vegetable oil in a nice size frying pan or deep fryer. Rinse your pork chops and dip in your batter and place in your frying pan or deep fryer. Flip in between frying if it starts to brown too soon reduce heat.

CHOPS AND RICE

Ingredients:
4 to 6 Pork Chops
1 to 2 cans of Italian Stewed tomatoes
Flour
Butter
Rice
Crisco Vegetable Oil

Directions:
Season some flour with Lawry's Seasoning Salt, Pepper and Garlic Powder. To fry your pork chops

Butter a nice size baking pan

Pour uncooked rice in the pan

Rinse your pork chops then dip them on both sides in the flour and fry.

Heat some oil enough to fry your pork chops. Not hard or crispy but until your chops or fully cooked. Place fried pork chops on top of rice, then pour the Italian stewed tomatoes and juice over the top of the pork chops. Fill the empty can with water and pour over the contents in the pan. Use a fork and lift the pork shops enough for the water to get down to the rice. You can cut the tomatoes in half or into smaller pieces. Cover with foil and bake at 350 degrees until rice is fully cooked. If your rice is not fully cooked add more water if needed and return to the oven and bake until done.

I serve with Broccoli or Italian cut Green Beans and Cornbread. Delicious!

YOU CAN DO IT
MAKE YOUR OWN ENCHILADA SAUCE

Ingredients:
2 tablespoons olive oil
2 tablespoons flour
¼ cup chili powder
½ teaspoon garlic powder
½ teaspoon ground cumin
¼ teaspoon dried oregano
2 cups chicken stock
1 can of Wolf Brand Chili
4 oz can of tomato sauce or tomato paste spoon in to taste (optional)
Salt optional

Directions:
Heat oil in a saucepan. Add flour and cook for a few minutes, whisking constantly. Add in the chili powder, garlic powder, cumin, oregano and Chili, cook for 1 more minute, whisking constantly.

Reduce heat and gradually pour in the chicken stock, whisking until no lumps. Let simmer whisking constantly for about 5 to 10 minutes, uncovered until the sauce is slightly thick. Season to taste.

BEEF ENCHILADAS

Ingredients:
Flour or Corn Tortillas
1 Onion
3 lb. ground meat
3 8 0z. Cans of tomato sauce
3 Packs of Enchilada sauce mix
1Texas Block Chili or 2 cans of Wolf Brand no beans Chili
Mild Cheddar and Fiesta Mix Shredded Cheese

Directions:
Preheat your oven to 350 degrees

Cook your ground beef with chopped onions, drain your grease and set aside. In a saucepan mix the 3 packs of enchilada mix with 1½ cups of water, heat and stir well. Then add the 3 cans of tomato sauce and the block chili. Add more water if your sauce seems too thick. Then add ½ or ¾ of the sauce to the meat and stir.

Spoon a desired amount of meat into the tortilla shell then roll and place in your baking pan and repeat. The remaining enchilada sauce, pour over your enchiladas and sprinkle some cheese on the top and cover with foil. Bake on 350 until the cheese melts.

THE FRIED CHICKEN

Ingredients:
Chicken Wings (any chicken parts)
Deep Fryer and Basket
Cooking Oil
Flour (optional) I season my flour
Seasoning (I use Lawry's, Garlic Powder, Pepper and Accent)

Directions:
Heat oil 375 to 400 degrees

Using flour pour in a bowl and season flour with seasonings listed above. Coat the chicken wings in the seasoned flour. (no flour season chicken and fry).

Place wings in the basket and place in the deep fryer. Cook until golden brown and crispy. (using skillet heat oil carefully place one at a time in the skillet, Reduce heat if cooking too fast. Turn chicken wings over with a fork and cook until meat runs clear, tender and crispy) I remove and let drain on paper towels.

MAKE YOUR OWN
BUFFALO HOT WING SAUCE

Ingredients:
Chicken Wings
Butter
Louisiana Hot Sauce
Brown Sugar

Directions:
Deep fry or bake chicken

Add 2 tablespoon of butter, a pinch of brown sugar, and add hot sauce (as much as you like to taste) in a saucepan or in a microwaveable bowl and heat until butter melts and stir, continue to add any ingredients to taste. Great for dipping fried chicken wings or pour over chicken and toss.

A PARTIES CROCK POT FAVORITE
BBQ MEATBALLS

Ingredients:
Crock pot
1 to 2 bags of Great Value Homestyle Meatballs
2 Bottles of Kraft Sweet Honey bbq sauce (I use 1 Sweet Honey and 1 Spicy Honey) 2 Bell peppers
1 Onion

Directions:
Pour meatballs in your crock pot, pour bbq sauce over meatballs, cut up bell pepper and onions in large pieces, (or any size you like) put in the crock pot. Toss until everything is coated. Cover and heat. Add more sauce if needed.

This one I serve with Hawaiian Rolls. A great party favorite.

QUICK AND EASY MEATBALL SUBS

Ingredients:
1 to 2 bags of Great Value Meatballs Italian Style
2 Jars of Ragu Chunky Mushroom Sauce or any Marinara Sauce
1 bag of shredded parmesan cheese
1 bag of shredded mozzarella cheese
Hoagie buns (I sometimes use regular hotdog buns)
Butter

Directions:
Meatballs are already pre-cooked.

Pour meatballs and sauce in a pot over medium heat, stirring while heating making sure the sauce covers and coats the meatballs.

Reduce heat, let simmer while you toast your buns.

1. Placing a small amount of butter in a skillet on medium heat and placing the buns spreaded open but not apart, toast to your desired color.
2. Spread butter over the buns and place in a toaster or oven and cook until lightly toasted. Once that is done spoon meatballs and sauce on your buns as much as you like and garnish with cheese. (I place mine in the oven and let my cheese melt) Yummy

MOMMY'S
HOMEMADE BANANA NUT BREAD

Ingredients:
Bananas overly ripe
Eggs
Buttermilk
Vegetable Oil
Flour
Sugar
Salt
Baking Soda (Arm and Hammer)
Vanilla Flavor
Pecans or Walnuts
2 8 inch Loaf Pans or four 4 inch loaf pans **Directions:**
3 Overly Ripe Bananas
2 Eggs
¼ cup plus 2 Tablespoons of Buttermilk ¾ cup of vegetable oil
1 ¾ cup of flour.
1 ½ cup of sugar
½ teaspoon salt
1 teaspoon of baking soda (Arm and Hammer) 1 ½ teaspoon vanilla flavor
1 cup of pecans or walnuts

Directions:
Mix dry ingredients by hand. Add all wet ingredients vanilla and nuts. Bake at 325 degrees 45 to 50 minutes.

CHESS PIE

Ingredients:
Sugar
Yellow Corn Meal
Butter
Eggs
Vinegar
Vanilla Flavor
Homogenize Milk
Un-bake Deep Dish pie crust.

Directions:
Mix by hand ! With a spoon no mixer.

Mix 1 1/3 cup sugar, 2 tablespoon yellow corn meal, 1 stick of melted butter real good.

Then add eggs ONE AT A TIME. Makes a big difference Add 1 tablespoon of vinegar, 1 teaspoon vanilla flavor extract mix well. Add ¼ cup of milk.

OOOH! WEEE! CHOCOLATE PIE!

Ingredients:
1-¼ cup of sugar
½ cup of plain flour
¼ cup of Cocoa
Dash of Salt
4 egg yolks
2 cups of milk
¼ cup of butter
1 tsp of vanilla
1-9" Deep pie crust

Directions:
Bake pie crust until golden
Combine first 4 ingredients in a saucepan;
Set aside.
Combine milk and egg yolks.
Stir milk and egg yolks into mixture; add butter.
Cook over medium heat, and stir constantly until the mixture thickens and boils.
Remove from heat; stir in vanilla; spoon into pie crust.
Meringue:
Use the 2 egg whites
4 tablespoon of sugar
½ teaspoon vanilla
Beat egg whites until frothy, gradually add sugar, continuing to beat until still peaks form add vanilla. Spread on top of pie.

AUNT KATHY'S BANANA PUDDING

Ingredients:
Bananas
2 Boxes Vanilla wafer cookies
Flour
Sugar
Salt
Eggs
2 Cans Carnation Milk
Homogenized Milk
Vanilla Flavor

Directions:
Sift ¾ cup of flour
2 cups of sugar
a pinch or two of salt

mix 8 egg yolks
2 cans of carnation milk
2 cans of homogenized milk (pour in carnation can)
1 tablespoon vanilla flavor extract.
In a bowl and combine to dry mixture.

Combine all dry goods in the pot you will be using to heat. Then combine one can of milk, eggs, and flavor in a separate bowl. Add the two and stir until mixed well then add remaining cans of milk. Cook on medium to low heat and stir continuously. Add more milk if the pudding gets too thick.

MY BEST FRIEND PAMELA'S WHIPPING POUND CAKE

Ingredients:
3 cups of Sugar
3 cups of flour
6 eggs
1 ½ teaspoon vanilla extract
1 teaspoon lemon extract
½ pint whipping cream
2 sticks of butter(I use salted Land O Lakes)

Directions:
Blend all dry ingredients in a nice size bowl and in another bowl blend all the liquids, blend well. Then pour dry goods in with your liquids and mix well until smooth. Butter and flour a Bundt pan (optional use the non-stick baking sprays).

Bake at 350 degrees for an hour, or until golden brown. Insert a tooth-pick before removing the cake from the pan. If the toothpick does not pull clean, place the cake back in the center of your oven and let it cook a little more, until your toothpick comes out clean

MRS. MELBA'S DELICIOUS
PEANUT PATTIES

Ingredients:
2 Cups Sugar
½ Cup Water
½ Cup Light Karo Syrup
2 Cups of Raw Peanuts
1 Tablespoon Butter
½ tsp Vanilla
4 or 5 drops of Red Food Coloring

Directions:
Butter a cookie sheet

Mix together Sugar, Water and Karo Syrup, microwave for 3 minutes. Add peanuts and microwave for 10 to 11 minutes.

Add remaining ingredients, stir until mixture begins to thicken and turn creamy looking. Drop a teaspoon size of your mixture onto the buttered cookie sheet. (Be careful your mixture will be very hot.)

7 UP CAKE

Have all ingredients at room temperature

Ingredients:
3 cups sugar
3 cups flour
2 sticks butter
½ cup butter flavor solid crisco
6 eggs
¾ cup 7-up soda
1 teaspoon lemon flavor extract
2 teaspoon vanilla flavor extract
1 teaspoon butter flavor extract

Directions:
Cream together sugar, butter and Crisco. Add flour and eggs alternately to the mixture and mix. Add extracts and add 7-up last and mix.

Bake at 325 degrees for 55-60 minutes in a Bundt pan. Spray Bundt pan with Pam or grease with butter and flour.

Icing:

Mix some of the leftover 7-up and powdered sugar in a bowl and mix well. Add more powdered sugar to thicken and drizzle over your cake.

BUTTERY CHEWS
(COOKIES)

Ingredients:
¾ cup (1 ½ sticks) unsalted butter, softened 1 cup granulated sugar
1 large egg
1 large egg yolk
2 ½ teaspoon vanilla extract
2 ¼ cups all purpose flour
¼ cup cornstarch
1 teaspoon baking soda
½ teaspoon sea salt

Directions:
Preheat oven to 350 degrees and line baking sheets with parchment paper (wax paper)

Place the butter and sugar in a large mixing bowl and beat on medium -high speed until very pale and fluffy (about 3 to 5 minutes) Add the egg and beat on medium high speed until mixed well. Stir in the egg yolk and vanilla extract mix well. Scrape the bottom and sides of the bowl with a silicone spatula, then add the flour, cornstarch, baking soda and salt. Stir together until mixed well.

Use a 1 or 1.5 tablespoon cookie scoop to drop balls of cookie dough on the baking sheets spacing about two inches apart. Flatten the balls slightly with the spatula. Bake the cookies (one sheet at a time) in the center of the oven rack for 8 to 12 minutes or until the edges are set and beginning to turn light golden brown.

PEANUT BUTTER CAKE

Ingredients:
1 Box of Yellow cake mix (I prefer Duncan Hines)
1 Vanilla Instant Pudding mix
4 Eggs
1 Cup.of Milk
1/4 Cup of Butter
1Cup peanut butter

Directions:
Combine all ingredients in a large mixer bowl. Blend; then beat at medium speed for 5 minutes. Pour in a greased and floured 10-inch baking pan. Bake at 350 degrees for 55-60 minutes or until cake if firm. Cool for 15 minutes.

ICING:
Mix 1 room temperature stick of butter, 1 1//2 teaspoon of vanilla, 1 table-spoon of peanut butter or (if you want a crunchy icing use the crunchy peanut butter}, 1/4 cup milk, and 1 cup confectioners' sugar. If your icing seems to be too thick, you can add more milk, If you think it's too thin you can add more sugar;

QUICK & EASY HOT CARAMEL APPLE PIE

Ingredients:
Deep Dish pie crust
2 cans of Apple Filling
1 Box of Pillsbury Pie Crust
1 Stick of Butter
Cinnamon
Caramel Syrup
Sugar

Directions:
Pour apple filling into pie crust and add ½ a stick of butter. Roll out your pie crust and cover pie pinching all around the edges on top. Cut four slits starting in the center of the pie crust out to an angle.

Melt the rest of the butter adding a pinch of cinnamon and 1//2 teaspoon of sugar. Cinnamon & Sugar optional. Then spread over the top of the pie.

Bake at 275 for 30 minutes or until the pie crust is golden brown. Drizzle Caramel over the top. Serve with vanilla ice cream.

STRAWBERRY CHEESECAKE MY WAY

Ingredients:
2 Philadelphia Cream Cheese
2 eggs
I/2 cup of sugar
3/4 teaspoon of vanilla flavor
Graham cracker crust pie shell 6 oz. or 9 oz. I prefer Nabisco
Strawberry Gel Glaze I prefer Marie's or Martinez brand

Directions:
Mix all ingredients until smooth. Mix on medium.

(Philadelphia Cream Cheese mix best when it's room temperature.)

Pour filling into the pie crust and bake for 40 to 45 min. 325 degrees or until firm. Let cool then add your Strawberry Glaze and top with strawberries.

If you want to make two at one time just double the ingredients, but make sure it is mixed well no lumps.

ICED COFFEE
SHERRY'S FAVORITES WILL BECOME
SOME OF YOURS

Ingredients:

1 ½ cups of strong hot brewed coffee

¼ cup caramel syrup, plus more for garnishing.

3 tablespoons sugar or to taste

Ice Cubes or coffee ice cubes

1 ½ cups of cold milk or half and half (I like Coffee Mate Vanilla Caramel Creamer too) Whipped Cream for garnish (Optional)

Directions:

After the coffee is finished brewing and is hot and fresh, pour 1/1/2 cups into a measuring cup. Stir in the caramel syrup. Melts and mix well while coffee is hot. If you add the caramel syrup straight into the measuring cup, and you are using a 2 cup measuring cup, pour in the caramel until it reaches 1 ¾ cup with the coffee, stir well.

Add your sugar and stir again until all sugar and caramel is dissolved completely

Place in the refrigerator and shill until cold. (I place my cup in the freezer or prepare the night before and place it in the fridge).When it's time to serve, pour your coffee over ice (coffee ice cubes add that extra flavor).

Add your milk or half and half to top the glass. And if you are pouring for two and you want that pretty perfect expensive coffee look, garnish with whipped cream and drizzle caramel syrup over the top.

The adult way (Optional Try it with Vodka or Rum and or Chocolate Syrup)

STRAWBERRY LEMONADE WITH A TWIST

Ingredients:
1 Bottle Pink Moscato
6 Cups of Lemonade
¼ Cups of Strawberry Vodka
Frozen Strawberry Slices
Lemon Slices

Directions:
Mix in large pitcher
Add more of each to taste.

LEMONADE GONE WILD

Ingredients:
1 cup Countrytime Lemonade Mix
2 cups cold water
1 can of chilled pineapple juice. (I use the 46 oz) 2 cans chilled Sprite

Directions:
Mix and pour over ice optional add lemons to garnish.

WHITE WINE SANGRIA YOUR WAY

Ingredients:
2 bottles white wine
3 shots of gin
½ bottle ginger ale
Orange juice to taste
1 plim
1 kiwi
Handful raspberries
Handful blackberries

Directions:
Chop the plum and kiwi. Mash the berries, add to a Sangria jug, along with wine, gin, ginger ale and orange juice. Allow to sit for 2 to 3 hours before serving.

By Popular Demand
KOOL AID PICKLES

Ingredients:
1 Jar Pickles (I prefer the large jar of Best Maid Pickles) Dill or Sour.
2 to 3 cups os sugar
Cayenne pepper
3 to 4 pkgs of Tropical Punch Kool-Aid. (experiment with any flavor Kool aid)

Directions:
Pour pickle juice into a nonstick pot

On low heat add 3 cups of sugar, packs of Kool aid a dash of cayenne pepper or as much as you like to taste if you want them really spicy.

Heat and stir until the sugar dissolves.

Remove pickles and slice them down the middle and place back in the jar. Pour the kool aid pickle juice back in the jar over the sliced pickles. Place the lid on loose until the juice cools down and then tighten the lid and let the jar of pickles sit for a week. Yes they are the best if you let them marinate for a week. Yes 7 days then enjoy

This is when you know the pickles are ready to eat is when the inside of the pickles are the same color of the Kool aid.

Thank you from my
HEART

A very special thanks to my mother Gloria who first taught me not only how to cook but how to cook with love, which consists of preparation and how to make it appealing to the eye.

To my husband Joseph S for always supporting me in all of my endeavors, and for always encouraging me to try different foods.

To my sister Antoinette for always cheering me on and making sure I have everything together. Thank you for being my number one fried chicken fan and for being the best big sister ever.

I want to thank my daughter Michelle for never giving up on me and pushing me to do this cookbook to have to pass down in our family. I began teaching you how to cook at an early age. Now seeing you cook for your family does my heart good.

To my son Joseph A who I call the chef. You have really gone above and beyond. You are a beast at roasted vegetables, sauteing and stir fry meals amongst other things.

To my niece LaNae who also inspired me to do this cookbook and to think all you wanted was French fries. Now you have a family of your own, cooking for two football players (your boys).

To my Aunt Kathy aka Auntie who always made time to answer any questions I may have about a dish and walk me through it.

In loving memory of my aunt Johnnie Bell who taught me how to make the best cornbread dressing ever.

In loving memory of my aunt Nancy who taught me how to bake the most delicious pies ever.

Thanks to all of friends who have waited patiently for years for me finish this cookbook and to all of you who have purchased my cookbook, I hope it brings joy and love to your table.- Sherry BON APPETIT!